PHAR LAP

A True Legend

Phar Lap at Melbourne Museum, 2001
PHOTOGRAPHER: JOHN BROOMFIELD (MV)

Michael Reason

PHAR LAP

A True Legend

Victoria
The Place To Be

museum
VICTORIA

Published by Museum Victoria, 2005
Text © Museum Victoria, 2005
Images © Museum Victoria unless
otherwise noted or out of copyright.

We have made every effort to obtain
copyright and moral permission for use
of all images. Please advise of any errors
or omissions.

History & Technology Department
Museum Victoria
GPO Box 666E
Melbourne
Victoria 3001
Australia

www.museum.vic.gov.au

CHIEF EXECUTIVE OFFICER:
Dr J. Patrick Greene

DIRECTOR, COLLECTIONS, RESEARCH
AND EXHIBITIONS:
Dr Robin Hirst

HEAD, HISTORY & TECHNOLOGY
DEPARTMENT:
Dr Richard Gillespie

AUTHOR:
Michael Reason

DESIGN:
Propellant

PRINTED BY:
Hyde Park Press, Adelaide, South Australia

NATIONAL LIBRARY OF AUSTRALIA
CATALOGUING-IN-PUBLICATION DATA:
  Reason, Michael.
  Phar Lap: a true legend.
  ISBN 0 9577471 9 5.
  1. Phar Lap (Race horse).
  2. Race horses – Australia – Biography.
  3. Horse racing – Australia.
  I. Museum Victoria.
  II. Title.

  798.400994

Form Guide

Race record	51 starts: 37 wins, three seconds and two thirds
Stake money	£56,425, plus US$50,000
Breeding	Night Raid–Entreaty (by Winkie)
Foaled	Timaru, New Zealand, 4 October 1926
Died	Menlo Park, California, 5 April 1932
Owners	D. J. Davis and H. R. Telford
Trainer	H. R. Telford
Colour	Chestnut (near red)
Height	17.1 hands
Biggest wins	Agua Caliente Handicap
	Melbourne Cup
	AJC Derby
	Victoria Derby
	W. S. Cox Plate (twice)
Race colours	1929–30 Red jacket, black and white hooped sleeves, red cap
	1931–32 Red jacket, red and green hooped sleeves, black cap

LEFT: The museum received four of Phar Lap's prize winning sashes as part of the Telford family donations in the 1990s.

MUSEUM VICTORIA COLLECTION
PHOTOGRAPHER: JOHN BROOMFIELD (MV)

Phar Lap, c.2000

Renowned Aboriginal artist Jimmy Pike knew little of the jockey he was named after until a few years before his death. He painted this interpretation of the Phar Lap legend, placing the horse against the landscape of his Western Australian home.

Contents

This 1932 image of Phar Lap's sire (father) Night Raid, was donated to the museum in 2000. The donor's father had worked for A. F. Roberts, the breeder of Phar Lap, during the 1930s.

CHAPTER 1

Lot 41: The Foal from Timaru

For over 70 years, Australians have flocked to Museum Victoria to see their beloved Phar Lap. Although those who lived through his short life diminish with every year, people still come to the museum especially to see him, and he is considered by many as its number one drawcard. Why are people drawn to him? Is it because of his unsurpassed racing record, or his status as a Melbourne icon? Or, is it simply because he is still such a magnificent creature and a high point in the art of taxidermy? It is nearly impossible to say why, but visiting Phar Lap has become an almost essential part of either living in or visiting Melbourne.

However, it was a far from magnificent sight that greeted trainer Harry Telford when Phar Lap first arrived in Australia in 1928. The horse could only be described as gangly to look at and awkward in movement when he was off-loaded at the Sydney docks, his appearance unlikely to inspire optimism in his future by those who saw him. His face was covered in warts, and there was little indication of the champion that he was destined to become.

Telford had been around horses his whole life, with his father training them for a living, first in Ballarat and then near Wellington in New Zealand. Harry had been fascinated by pedigree charts from an early age, and spent many hours studying them to see if he could discover what made a champion. A career as a trainer seemed inevitable, and he moved to Sydney and established himself in business with a small but loyal clientele.

By the mid-1920s, and in his fifties, Telford was yet to train that elusive winner he had dreamed about since his days in Ballarat. By now he had a wife and a young son to support, so finding a prospective champion was more critical than ever. Then one day he stumbled across a yearling in the catalogue for the 1927 Trentham sales in New Zealand. He had been poring over pedigree charts, and felt sure he had found a potential winner in the one-year-old colt known as 'Lot 41'. Ever protec-

One of the star items in the museum's Phar Lap collection is this set of racing colours donated by the family of Harry Telford. These were the colours that Phar Lap's jockeys wore while he was leased by Telford during 1929 and 1930.

MUSEUM VICTORIA COLLECTION
PHOTOGRAPHER: JOHN BROOMFIELD (MV)

tive of his technique, Telford never revealed what drew him to this lot, but the horse's pedigree did include such illustrious champions as St Simon, Musket and — arguably Australia's greatest racehorse up until then — the 1890 Melbourne Cup winner Carbine.

Lot 41 was foaled at the Seadown stud in Timaru, New Zealand. His sire Night Raid had originally raced in England and, after a mediocre career in Australia, was sold to the stud's owner A. F. Roberts, after breaking down in Melbourne. Suitable only for breeding purposes, Night Raid served a number of mares at Seadown, including one named Entreaty. From this pairing, a chestnut colt was born on 4 October 1926.

Telford's lack of success had left him and his business in a financial mess. He knew he would never be able to afford to buy Lot 41 but, convinced of the horse's potential, he approached one of his clients David J. Davis with a proposal. An American-born entrepreneur, Davis had made a fortune through his import and photography businesses, and used this to finance his passion for horse racing. Telford suggested that Davis buy the horse and bring it back to Sydney for him to train. Davis already owned a number of horses, and it took Telford weeks to convince him that the horse's 'exceptional breeding' warranted his investment.

ABOVE: Many people tried to discover the secret of Phar Lap's success by compiling detailed pedigree charts such as this one, which contains the names of ten generations of his forbears.
MUSEUM VICTORIA COLLECTION

LEFT: The famous triumvirate: Jim Pike, Phar Lap and Tommy Woodcock.

Davis finally relented after much badgering by Telford, and arranged for a business associate to bid on his behalf. He was authorised to bid up to 190 guineas, and the horse was knocked down to him for what Telford considered the bargain price of 160 guineas. Harry's brother Hugh, a horse trainer in New Zealand, had inspected the colt before auction and afterwards arranged for him to be transported to Sydney.

The horse's less than desirable appearance tested even Harry Telford's convictions when he laid eyes on him at the docks. If Telford was slightly disappointed with the animal, Davis was furious when he was shown the unbecoming colt that he had purchased and paid to have shipped over from New Zealand. He decided there and then that he had wasted enough of his money on this creature and declared that he wanted nothing more to do with it. Unable to repay the 160 guineas, Telford devised a leasing deal where he would cover the feeding and training costs and, in return, Davis would be entitled to one-third of any winnings. It is likely that, as Davis agreed to this, he would have been highly sceptical of ever making any money out of the arrangement — but how wrong could he be. ❧

As soon as he started winning races, a number of businesses attempted to cash in on the Phar Lap name. The Myona Cigar Company of Richmond produced this sheet of uncut lids for their branded tobacco.

CHAPTER 2

Bobby Boy: The Young Phar Lap

Telford set about breaking in and training his new charge almost immediately. Visitors to the stables in Kensington, near Randwick racecourse, during 1928 were unimpressed with the colt's early form, and he was described by one as looking more like a ragged kangaroo dog than a potential race winner. He appeared too lazy and docile to be given any chance of becoming the champion on which Telford had risked his business and his reputation. Telford knew that he would have to take drastic action to mould the colt into the success that he could surely become.

The first task was to have the horse gelded. Gelding, or castration, removes the influence of testosterone on the colt, making him more manageable and assisting with his concentration as he learns to focus on racing rather than on the young fillies around him. An early indication of Phar Lap's resilience and determination was observed by the vet after the operation who, on seeing the horse head for a patch of lawn and begin grazing, said 'Put a saddle on him and you can ride him home. That one doesn't need any nursing'.

Telford's other plan was to initiate a rigorous and gruelling training schedule, which included almost daily runs over towering coastal sand hills as a means of strengthening the colt's muscles by pushing them to their limits. Referred to by others as a form of 'sudden death' training, Telford was determined to make or break the gelding into a champion. Training in the sand hills also meant that he regularly avoided having to pay the shilling fee charged to use the track at Randwick, an important consideration for the cash-strapped trainer.

One person who watched Phar Lap's early track work with great interest was Dr Aubrey Moore Ping, a local physician who was to play a small but pivotal role in the story. Legend has it that Ping was asked one day by Telford what the word for 'lightning' was in his native language. Ping's mother was Scottish, but his father was Chinese and had taught him some Zhuang, a language spoken in southern China. Telford wrote down the answer as 'Phar Lap', with a 'Ph' rather than the simple 'F', and split into two words to replicate the dominant pattern set by the names of previous Melbourne Cup winners. As Zhuang shares many words with the Thai language, including that for lightning, it was later mistakenly reported that Phar Lap was named by a Thai speaker.

So it was with a Chinese name that Phar Lap was registered in Sydney on 3 December 1928, ironically at a time when the federal government's White Australia Policy severely restricted the movement of Asian people, and their cultural influence, into Australia. However, it was by a far less exotic Anglo nickname that Phar Lap came to be known by those around him, a name bestowed on him by the person who became arguably his closest friend and companion. Bobby Boy, or Bobby for short, was the name given to him by strapper Tommy Woodcock who felt an immediate affinity with the horse from their first meeting.

BELOW: Phar Lap with his strapper, Tommy Woodcock, at Sol Green's farm at Bacchus Marsh, 1929.
MUSEUM VICTORIA COLLECTION

OPPOSITE PAGE: With no trademark laws, companies were able to apply Phar Lap's image to a whole range of products, such as this cake tin, without having to pay a penny to his owners.
MUSEUM VICTORIA COLLECTION
PHOTOGRAPHER: MICHELLE MCFARLANE

LEFT: Phar Lap and jockey Jim Pike after their victory in the 1929 AJC Derby at Randwick. The race was also notable as Pike's debut ride on Phar Lap.
MUSEUM VICTORIA COLLECTION

OPPOSITE PAGE: Certificate of registration of racehorse, 1928
MUSEUM VICTORIA COLLECTION

Aaron 'Tommy' Woodcock was born in country New South Wales in 1905. Moving to Sydney as a teenager to train as an apprentice jockey at Randwick, he tasted success early, winning his first race at 16, and became a freelance rider after completing his apprenticeship in 1923. He kept riding until 1927, but his height and burgeoning weight made it increasingly difficult for him to find work. Always the optimist, he decided to make the most of his love of horses in the role of a strapper, who was engaged to take care of a horse's every need, including grooming, feeding requirements and even mucking out the stables.

Woodcock worked on and off for a number of trainers at Randwick, including Telford, and he was there the day that Phar Lap arrived from New Zealand. It was after a sand hill run, when he found Phar Lap hot, sweaty and tied up in his stable, that the seeds of their relationship were sown. Woodcock untied him, cleaned him up and let him rest for half an hour. From that

day onwards, Phar Lap saw Tommy as a generous and caring person, always ready with a kind word or a sugar cube treat. Although never a sentimental man, Telford witnessed the growing bond between Woodcock and Bobby Boy and recognised its importance to the horse's development. Woodcock continued working for other trainers, as Telford was unable to afford him full time, but Tommy always made sure he had time for his favourite charge and was available whenever Telford needed him.

In 1929 Phar Lap was entered in his first race, the aptly named Nursery Handicap at Sydney's Rosehill racecourse. He was ridden by 15-year-old apprentice Cashy Martin. The result was not the most illustrious of starts to what was to become a distinguished career: '… and Phar Lap last', announced a small report in the *Sydney Morning Herald* the next day. Telford was not too concerned with this result; he looked upon Phar Lap's early races as part of the training process, and was

No. **B179**

CERTIFICATE OF
REGISTRATION OF RACEHORSE.

This is to Certify *that the following particulars have been duly Registered for the*

Racehorse named   PHAR LAP.

Color and Sex   Chestnut Gelding.

Age   2 years.

Brands and Distinguishing Marks (in full)   Unbranded.   Near hind leg and fetlock
white off hind coronet white, white star on forehead, four black
spots on off quarter, white spot over black spot near quarter.

Pedigree (Sire)   Night Raid.   (Dam)   Entreaty.

Name and Address of Owner   Mr. D. J. Davis,

Clarence Street, Sydney, N.S.W.

W Goddard Spville
Registrar.

Date   3rd. December, 1928.

ABOVE: Like Father Christmas bringing joy to poor children in a Melbourne slum, Phar Lap's success also brought smiles to the faces of those affected by the Depression.

PHOTOGRAPHER: F. OSWALD BARNETT
F. OSWALD BARNETT COLLECTION,
STATE LIBRARY OF VICTORIA

TOP RIGHT: Advances in action photography enabled newspapers to capture Phar Lap's impressive running style.

RIGHT: Away from the track, Phar Lap was treated almost as a beloved family pet by those around him. Here he is with trainer Harry Telford's young son Gerald pretending to ride him to victory.

MUSEUM VICTORIA COLLECTION

"PHAR LAP" with MASTER G.H.TELFORD Up

not expecting positive results so soon. This was just as well, as the horse was unplaced in his next three races.

It wasn't until the Maiden Juvenile Handicap at Rosehill on 27 April that Phar Lap had his first taste of success. Telford had searched through the racing calendar for weeks, trying to decide on a suitable race to enter the horse in. He wanted one which Phar Lap would have a reasonable possibility of winning, but with other chances in it which would ensure fair betting odds on his horse. As well as being a racing man, Telford was also a gambling man, so a win would mean a large dividend, and two-thirds share of the prize purse. Phar Lap's win delivered him both.

Telford rested Phar Lap over the next few months, before producing him as a full-grown three-year-old. Phar Lap lost his next five races, but several factors had changed since the earlier losses. He was now racing against a better standard of competitor — some of the best three-year-olds in Sydney. Telford also decided to try Phar Lap over a distance rather than as a sprinter. This paid off when he ran a sizzling second in the Chelmsford Stakes at Randwick on 14 September. The racing fraternity finally took notice of him and of his trainer, and in his next race, the Rosehill Guineas, he was named favourite (as would be the case in all but one of his future races, including three consecutive Melbourne Cups). Phar Lap won with ease, silencing his critics and gaining public adulation and acclaim as the newest champion of the turf.

His next race, the AJC Derby, was another impressive win, and the beginning of another important partnership. Jim Pike rode Phar Lap to victory, their first of 27 victories in 30 races — a truly extraordinary feat. Pike was regarded by many as the star rider of his time. His only problem was his above average weight for a jockey, which meant that he was continually having to starve himself and spend hours at the Turkish baths to meet the weight requirements. When Pike was unable to lose enough weight to ride, Telford would employ another jockey such as the well regarded Bill Elliot.

Phar Lap's early successes coincided with the onset of the worldwide economic downturn beginning with the October 1929 crash of the New York stock exchange, that became known as the Great Depression. With falling overseas prices for Australian commodities such as wheat and wool, farmers and other business people saw a swift decrease in their earnings. As businesses collapsed, many people found themselves out of work, with more than a quarter of the workforce unemployed by 1932. With no government assistance program in place as there is today, they had to rely on charities and food hand-outs. The unemployed and their families faced hardship and eviction, and life became bleak for many Australians. They had lost faith in the government's ability to lead, and were calling out for a hero.

No-one could predict that this hero would come equipped with hooves, a tail and a brown silky mane. Between September 1929 and March 1932, Phar Lap won 36 of his 46 races, running unplaced in only one. Although his odds were often small, a bet on him was one of the few positive 'sure things' left in life during the Depression. It's no wonder that during this time Phar Lap became the 'hero to a nation'. ❧

Trainer Harry Telford and son Gerald at the presentation of the 1930 Melbourne Cup.
Herald, 5 November 1930

CHAPTER 3

The Coast of Melbourne

By the spring of 1929, with several wins under his belt, Telford decided it was time to shift his operation down south to Melbourne, home of Australia's most illustrious race — the Melbourne Cup. Recognising Tommy Woodcock's important role in Phar Lap's success, Telford offered the strapper a full-time position. Woodcock jumped at the opportunity to spend his days with his beloved Bobby. He didn't move from Phar Lap's side for the whole 36 hour journey from Sydney, even sleeping with him in his stock carriage, until they reached his new stables at Caulfield racecourse.

With Phar Lap unsettled and in far from peak form after the move and the onset of a cold, he and Jim Pike still managed to win the first major race of the Cup carnival, the Victoria Derby. Unfortunately, the horse's light weight as a three-year-old meant that Pike was too heavy to ride him in the Melbourne Cup three days later, and was replaced by local jockey Bobby Lewis. Unlike Pike, he had no experience with the feisty young horse and found him a real handful to ride. Still, he managed a credible third place to Nightmarch, another son of Night Raid, an indication of the greater things which were to follow.

This success enabled Telford to afford to lease Braeside, a large property at Mordialloc in south-eastern Melbourne. After resting over summer, Phar Lap made his first appearance for 1930 in the St George Stakes at Caulfield. He was again ridden by Bobby Lewis into third place, but the race is more notable as the first encounter between Phar Lap and another champion, the seven-year-old gelding Amounis who had built up an impressive record over the previous five years. Amounis would be the only horse to beat Phar Lap during his 21 races in 1930, achieving this feat twice.

Phar Lap went on to win a number of prestigious Victorian races that season, including the VRC St Leger Stakes, the Governor's Plate and the King's Plate (by 20 lengths). He then headed back to Sydney where he impressed sports journalists and others in the industry with his improved form and physical presence. His first start in the Chipping Norton Stakes at Warwick Farm again pitted him against several well regarded champions, including Amounis, Nightmarch and Chide. First Nightmarch, then Amounis, tried to overtake him, but

he outclassed the opposition, with the Sydney crowd cheering him as loudly as had the adoring crowds in Melbourne; his celebrity status had now spread across state borders. As with many other celebrities, Phar Lap's public showed their affection by bestowing a number of nicknames on him, including Big Red and the Red Terror, a reference to both his towering presence and his breathtaking speed on the track.

He easily won his next two races, the AJC St Leger and the Cumberland Stakes, but it was the 1930 AJC Plate at Randwick which is regarded by those who saw it as his greatest victory. The *Truth* acclaimed him as the 'Greatest Horse Ever' after this run, when he and Bill Elliot seemed to leave the ground and literally fly around the course. He again beat Melbourne Cup winner Nightmarch, but this time by an amazing 10 lengths. His time over the first two miles, at 3 minutes 20.5 seconds, was fast enough to have won him every Melbourne Cup before 1950 and every Sydney Cup before 1971. Elliot actually slowed him down over the last quarter mile, so fearful was he for the horse's health, until Phar Lap was only cantering by the time he passed the winning post.

Telford followed this triumph with a trip to Adelaide to appear in three races: the Elder Stakes, the Adelaide Cup and the King's Cup. Phar Lap effortlessly won the first and third of these, but was controversially withdrawn from the Adelaide Cup at the last minute, disappointing the many fans who had come to see their hero. After returning to Victoria, Phar Lap was rested for several months before heading north once more, as a four-year-old, for the opening of the 1930 spring racing season in Sydney.

RIGHT: This specially weighted saddle was custom made for jockey Bill Elliot by Harry Telford. Purchased with assistance from the Commonwealth government's National Cultural Heritage Account and Racing Victoria.

MUSEUM VICTORIA COLLECTION
PHOTOGRAPHER: RODNEY START (MV)

BELOW: The introduction of colour printing in newspapers enabled them to produce free souvenirs for their readers, such as this print celebrating Phar Lap's Agua Caliente victory.

MUSEUM VICTORIA COLLECTION

THE WINNER OF THE
AGUA CALIENTE HANDICAP.

W. Elliot,
Phar Lap's rider.

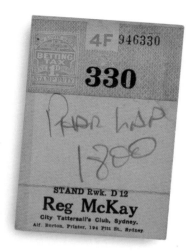

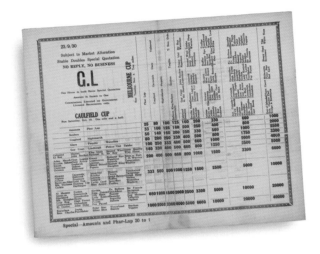

Even with the small odds on offer, punters were still willing to hand over large amounts of money to the bookies. This ticket is from Phar Lap's win in the Chelmsford Stakes at Randwick in 1930.

1930 Caulfield and Melbourne Cups Doubles Chart. The controversial scratching of Phar Lap from the Caulfield Cup proved an unpopular action amongst the Australian public.

Phar Lap and Jim Pike won five of their six races, losing only the first, the Warwick Stakes, to the now eight-year-old Amounis, with Nightmarch third. This win elevated Amounis to the favourite for the Caulfield Cup in October. However, doubt was emerging about whether Phar Lap would run in the Cup, to be held only a week after his final race in Sydney. Nightmarch had already been scratched and had returned to New Zealand, the rumour being that the owner was tired of his horse always being the bridesmaid to the Big Red bride. Bookmakers and punters were keen to find out if Phar Lap was running, as it was common practice to lay a double bet on the winners of both the Caulfield and Melbourne Cups.

On the Monday before the Caulfield Cup, Telford surprised everyone by scratching Phar Lap from the race,

not long before the deadline. The reason for this has never been clear. Was it because Telford was worried about overworking Phar Lap before the Melbourne Cup, or was it because people associated with the horse had bet heavily on an Amounis/Phar Lap Cups double? Whatever the reason, it was an unpopular move with the bookies and the public alike. Phar Lap ran one more race before Melbourne Cup week, an easy victory in the W. S. Cox Plate at Moonee Valley, but met with an unprecedentedly hostile response from the crowd and was even booed as he left the track.

The depth of these emotions may be behind the terrifying incident which occurred a week later, in the early hours of Derby Day. Around a quarter to six, Tommy Woodcock was on a pony walking Phar Lap back to

Melbourne Cup program, 1930
MUSEUM VICTORIA COLLECTION

A freelance press photographer captured some of the drama of Derby Day, 1930 in his annotated program. One of his notes reads "Phar Lap going home with 2 policemen".
MUSEUM VICTORIA COLLECTION

the stables after his morning work-out at Caulfield racecourse. Suddenly a car appeared with two shadowy occupants, a shotgun was drawn and a single shot rang out. Woodcock pushed Phar Lap against a fence, putting himself between the horse and the car. The blast understandably spooked them all, with Woodcock being dragged from the pony as he held on tight to Phar Lap's reins.

A witness to this frightening scene was a teenage boy, Robert Philpots, who kept what he had seen to himself until he decided to recount the story to staff at Museum Victoria in 2001:

> I was born and bred in Glenhuntly, and for my 14th birthday, which was in October 1930, I was given a bike from my cousin who had grown out

of it. He'd grown older and it was brought up to me on the Friday night …
Naturally I got up early on the Saturday morning to have a ride all round the streets, cause you could ride round streets in those days, cause of very few cars …
Anyway, I was riding up James Street, coming near the corner of Etna Street, when I saw Phar Lap and Tommy Woodcock coming down from Manchester Grove, and at that time there was a big black sedan car turned from James Street into Etna Street …
The next thing was — bang! … And this bloke in the back seat shot out a shotgun … it was only one blast from memory, and of course Tommy Woodcock — all the trainers in those days always

rode little ponies and led their horses — and of course he, he took the horse … up onto the footpath …

Then I, of course, got the wind up and went for my life and went down to the Ormond footy ground and stayed there for half an hour or so, till I got hungry for my breakfast and came home.

Whether this was a serious attempt on Phar Lap's life, or just designed to spook his owners into withdrawing him from the Cup, has never been established. There is inconclusive evidence on whether real shot or a blank was fired that morning. Regardless of the intent,

Phar Lap received around-the-clock protection from both his entourage and the police.
Argus, 3 November 1930

POLICE ESCORT FOR PHAR LAP.—After the attempt to shoot him on Saturday morning, Phar Lap, the Melbourne Cup favourite, left his stables at Glenhuntly in the afternoon with an escort of police motor-cyclists and plain-clothes constables.

Telford took the unsettling incident very seriously, as did the press with headlines such as 'Dastardly Attempt to Maim Cup Favourite'. He decided to keep Phar Lap in Derby Day's Melbourne Stakes, but with a security escort in tow, including plain-clothes detectives and motorcycle police, as the horse arrived to a hero's welcome. Whatever the effect on everyone else, the day's events seemed to have little on the star of the show as he went on to blitz the opposition and win by three lengths.

Telford decided not to take any more chances. Phar Lap went into hiding at St Albans, a property near Geelong, while a similar looking horse was used as a stand-in during training at Caulfield. Phar Lap was kept at St Albans until the morning of the Melbourne Cup, when a motor float arrived to take him to Flemington. There was more drama, as heavy rainfall affected the engine and it wouldn't start. After much sweating and cursing, the engine engaged and the entourage sped towards Flemington, arriving with less than an hour to spare — hardly enough time for the average horse to prepare for such a major race. As we have seen, though, Phar Lap was anything but average.

Often called 'the horse race that stops a nation', the Melbourne Cup has been run at Flemington every year since 1861, and has become the premier event in the Australian racing calendar. When American writer Mark Twain visited the Cup in 1895, he declared, 'Nowhere in the world have I encountered a festival of people that has such a magnificent appeal to the whole nation. The Cup astonishes me'.

By 1930, the Melbourne Cup carnival had been extended to four race days, covering the preceding Saturday and Cup Day, as well as the following Thursday and Saturday. Cup Day was still the major focus for the racing fraternity and public alike, and to win the Cup was the ultimate prize for owners and trainers. Phar Lap and Telford had missed out in 1929, while Jimmy Pike had ridden and lost the race 13 times before. Would it be theirs this time around?

After his late arrival, Phar Lap had to be fitted with his race shoes. He and Pike had a police escort in the mounting yard and to the starting boxes, even though it is highly unlikely that anyone would have tried anything sinister in front of thousands of witnesses and, more importantly, thousands of Phar Lap fans. The crowd was definitely on his side as the field burst from the starting gates and took off down the track. By the halfway mark, Temptation was almost four lengths clear. He soon tired, though, as the rest of the field caught up and overtook him. It wasn't until after the three-quarter mark that Pike made his move, and the crowd erupted as the familiar red cap and black and white hooped sleeves moved quickly through the field and hit the front. Despite being handicapped with a massive 9 stone 12 pounds (63 kilograms), and the toughest of opposition, Phar Lap passed the winning post three lengths clear of Second Wind.

Pike, Telford and Phar Lap were the toast of Flemington, if not the whole of Australia. Telford showed some rare emotion as he smiled and held aloft the prized trophy in one hand, his son proudly grasped in the other — public adulation was finally his. David Davis was happy to stay

The only way to see all the action from the track for those unable to attend was to visit the local cinema and watch the latest newsreels. This poster from the 1940s was used to entice people to rush along and see the Melbourne Cup on the big screen.
MUSEUM VICTORIA COLLECTION

in the background and let Telford have his day, although the money he is said to have made on his Amounis/Phar Lap Cups double bet would have explained the sly smile said to have lingered on his face.

Phar Lap's incredible win in the 1930 Cup only served to consolidate his position as 'the people's champion', but it was not by his remarkable form alone that he was able to achieve this. His momentous rise had coincided with significant changes to the mass media in Australia. These revolutions in radio, cinema and newspapers enabled the whole of the country, not just those who patronised its racecourses, to follow his rise to fame and share in his victories.

Newspapers were becoming easier to read, with bolder headlines, story introductions known as leads, and the placing of the important news story on the front page, rather than buried inside. Sports coverage doubled, even quadrupled, in most papers as editors realised its popular appeal, especially as competitions became organised along state and national lines. Photographs were increasingly important as technology improved and 'action photography' became more commonplace, enabling a horse race — particularly the finish — to be captured and presented to the world.

Fittingly, the oldest surviving Australian film is of the 1896 Melbourne Cup, but until the late 1920s the footage had been silent, which greatly hampered its ability to convey the excitement of race day. The first sound film *The Jazz Singer* was shown in Australia at the end of 1928, and by 1930 two-thirds of cinemas were equipped for sound. Newsreels — compilations of news, sport and

ABOVE: Even before the race had begun, the crowds were already cheering Phar Lap on. *Argus*, 5 November 1930

BELOW: The ease of Phar Lap's win in the 1930 Melbourne Cup is vividly captured in this presentation photograph, a memento treasured by the Telford family.
MUSEUM VICTORIA COLLECTION

THE ARGUS, WEDNESDAY, NOVEMBER 5, 1930.

TURNING INTO THE STRAIGHT.—A telephoto-lens picture of the Melbourne Cup field at the three-furlongs post. Muratti is on the rails, slightly ahead of Temptation, with Shadow King next on the left. Then Phar Lap in the centre and Carradale. Tregilla is just visible at the rear, behind Carradale.

The invention of the telephoto lens enabled photographers to capture some of the excitement of the running of the 1930 Melbourne Cup. Phar Lap is in the centre.
Argus, 5 November 1930

human interest stories — became an important part of the cinema experience. The second newsreel from Fox Movietone, Australia's first newsreel producer, was of the 1929 Melbourne Cup. Crowds rushed to see this, as well as Phar Lap's 1930 win and 1931 attempt, along with many of his other races which were captured on film, including his final run at Agua Caliente in Mexico.

Probably the most important of these media developments was the introduction of the radio into people's lives and homes. The first stations began broadcasting in 1923 but, as listeners had to hold a separate licence for each one, it was not until 1925 when a universal licence was introduced that the technology really took off. There were 1200 licence holders in 1924, exploding to 300,000 by 1929, then to 600,000 by 1933. As well as in private homes, radio sets appeared in public venues such as hotels, barber shops, billiard halls and social clubs. The first broadcast of a horse race was made from Adelaide's Cheltenham racecourse in 1925 and these grew so quickly in popularity that, by the time Phar Lap won the Melbourne Cup, the cheers of the thousands of spectators at Flemington were echoed around the nation by the hundreds of thousands of eager radio listeners.

Telford wanted to race Phar Lap in both the Linlithgow Stakes and the C. B. Fisher Plate, on the Thursday and Saturday after the Cup, although Woodcock was concerned that this was asking too much of even the great Phar Lap. He won both, even if his form had scared off most of the opposition, and he only raced against two other starters on the Saturday. This was the last race that Phar Lap would run under Telford's lease with Davis which was due to expire in February 1931. Telford, along with the rest of the country, was left wondering what his future involvement with the champion would be. ❧

Australians' last view of their champion was in November 1931, as he was loaded onto a ship bound for New Zealand. Little did they know they would never see him alive again.
MUSEUM VICTORIA COLLECTION

CHAPTER 4

Triumph Abroad

In December 1930, an important agreement was reached in Sydney between two business associates, if not friends. Davis offered to sell Telford a half share of Phar Lap for the seemingly bargain price of 4000 pounds. His motive was unclear, as Davis was a businessman above all else, but the results of this deal were much more obvious. From February 1931, Phar Lap's jockey would race in the new Telford/Davis colours of red jacket with red and green hooped sleeves, and a black cap.

Before he left for America, Phar Lap was rested at a property at Bacchus Marsh. He is seen here with a group of admirers including Tommy Woodcock and Harry Telford's son Gerald.

MUSEUM VICTORIA COLLECTION
PHOTOGRAPHER: MARK FRIEND

Phar Lap's first race under this new arrangement was the St George Stakes at Caulfield on St Valentine's Day. It would also be his first under the new handicap system introduced by the Victorian Racing Club at the beginning of the year for all its weight-for-age races, which penalised previously successful horses by increasing the weight they had to carry. He was to run in the Newmarket Handicap first, but a livid Telford withdrew him after he was asked to carry 11 stone 1 pound (70 kilograms). He won the St George with ease, but it was his next win that Jimmy Pike, amongst others, was to hail as his finest victory.

Phar Lap entered the Futurity Stakes at Caulfield carrying the maximum allowed for the race, 10 stone 3 pounds (65 kilograms), on a track soaked by heavy rain the previous night. It was also his first race of less than a mile in 18 months, so there were mixed expectations as to whether he could win over such a short distance. He missed the start, sitting in last place for most of the race, only powering up to first place in the last quarter. Pike reckoned that Phar Lap never ran harder or faster than he did on that day, to win by a neck — a win that catapulted him past his rival Amounis as the greatest Australian stakes winner ever.

He effortlessly won his next two races, but by then Pike, Woodcock and others were worried that Phar Lap was no longer in peak condition after what Pike described as his super-equine effort in the Futurity Stakes. His last race of the season, the C. M. Lloyd Stakes, was his first loss after 14 wins, and it was now obvious, even to Telford, that the horse was in desperate need of a long rest. The regular autumn trip to Sydney was cancelled

This photograph of Tommy Woodcock and Phar Lap was taken at Bacchus Marsh, in November 1931, just before Phar Lap headed to Sydney to begin his journey to New Zealand.

MUSEUM VICTORIA COLLECTION
PHOTOGRAPHER: MARK FRIEND

Total Stake and Purse Distribution Approximately One Million Dollars

Third Annual Winter Season 1931-1932

Thanksgiving Day to March Twenty-seventh Nineteen Thirty-two

Twenty-three Stake Events

Winner Agua Caliente Handicap Guaranteed $100,000

JAMES N. CROFTON
President

Mike Hall, Jockey O'Donnell up. Winner of 1931 Agua Caliente Handicap.

and Phar Lap was sent away to a property at Bacchus Marsh until late winter.

At first this disappointed Davis, who was hoping to show off his horse in front of his colleagues in Sydney, but his attention soon turned towards newer and richer pastures. Phar Lap had won almost every major Australian race, some twice, and had become somewhat of a large fish in a very small pond. England had been considered as a possible destination but, as geldings were excluded from most of the prestigious races, this was seen as a big financial risk. Not surprisingly, given his American

background and desire to eventually return there, Davis suggested the lucrative American circuit as Phar Lap's next potential conquest.

The richest prize of them all was the famed Agua Caliente Handicap, held just over the Mexican border near Tijuana. The $100,000 purse ensured that many of the world's best horses would be present. So keen were the members of the Agua Caliente Jockey Club to have Phar Lap as part of the 1932 field that they offered to partially fund his trip to Mexico, and open the way for him to be invited to run in other significant North American races. To Davis, this positive response was in stark contrast to the negative attitudes displayed towards him by the Victoria Racing Club and others. During a midyear business trip to America, a handshake was all it took to guarantee Phar Lap a place in the next year's race.

Meanwhile, Phar Lap had recuperated well under Woodcock's care, and was fit and ready for the beginning of the 1931 spring season. Two easy wins in Melbourne, including his debut at the now forgotten Williamstown racecourse, were followed by a triumphant return to Sydney where he blitzed the opposition with four starts for four wins. Australia's champion was back!

Rumours surfaced, first in the American press and then in Australia, that Phar Lap was heading to America at the end of the year. Davis was evasive when answering questions, as he knew it would not be a popular move in Australia, particularly amongst Phar Lap's thousands of adoring fans. These were the people who cheered in jubilation when he won the W. S. Cox Plate again, this time by two and a half lengths, in the perfect lead-up to the 1931 Melbourne Cup carnival.

Even after this convincing victory, Telford and Woodcock were already concerned about the possible effects of running Phar Lap in the Cup, with his allotted 10 stone 10 pounds (68 kilograms). Davis was less concerned, probably because he was keen to have his name attached to a Cup win. Pike reported that their next race, Derby Day's Melbourne Stakes, had been a very hard ride for them both, with the horse taking almost an hour to recover after winning by less than half a length. Telford was finally able to convince Davis to scratch the horse

ABOVE: Harry Telford had cherished this copy of the Agua Caliente Handicap Day program, signed to him by jockey Bill Elliot.
MUSEUM VICTORIA COLLECTION

OPPOSITE PAGE: The glamour and excitement of the Agua Caliente track is encapsulated in the booklet promoting the 1931–32 racing season, which culminated in the running of the Handicap in late March.
MUSEUM VICTORIA COLLECTION

from the Cup, reminding him that if Phar Lap broke down he would have no horse to take to America. However, the VRC, fearful of the effects of a late scratching of the favourite, convinced Davis — through persuasion or threat — to keep the horse in the race.

The Melbourne Cup started well enough for Phar Lap and he alternated between fourth, fifth and sixth position for most of the race. A late burst of speed brought a cheer from the crowd, but the celebratory mood was short-lived as he fell back to finish in eighth spot. He was entered in the C. B. Fisher Plate on the Saturday, but it was obvious to everyone that he was in no condition to run, and was scratched.

Davis took this occasion to announce to the world that Phar Lap would indeed be heading to North America to run in the 1932 Agua Caliente Handicap. An incredible prize purse and paid expenses made this an opportunity too good to miss. As his overseas expedition became the subject of debate around the country's dinner tables, Australians could not have known that their hero would never race in front of a home crowd again.

Telford was less keen than Davis about sending Phar Lap to America. He felt he had proved his ability, and from now on would be taken seriously as a trainer of champion racehorses. Besides, since his successes on the track, he had other potential winners at Braeside who

RIGHT: Although surrounded by impoverished neighbourhoods, the Agua Caliente racecourse and resort was a de luxe establishment.
MUSEUM VICTORIA COLLECTION

OPPOSITE PAGE: Harry Telford remained in Australia when Phar Lap went to America. Jockey Bill Elliot sent him this signed photograph as a memento of their triumph.
MUSEUM VICTORIA COLLECTION

Airplane view of the Agua Caliente Jockey Club. The grandstand is at the left with the Clubhouse and Paddock at the right. Beyond the green lawns of the infield are the stables of white Spanish stucco with red tile roofs.

Page Thirty-four

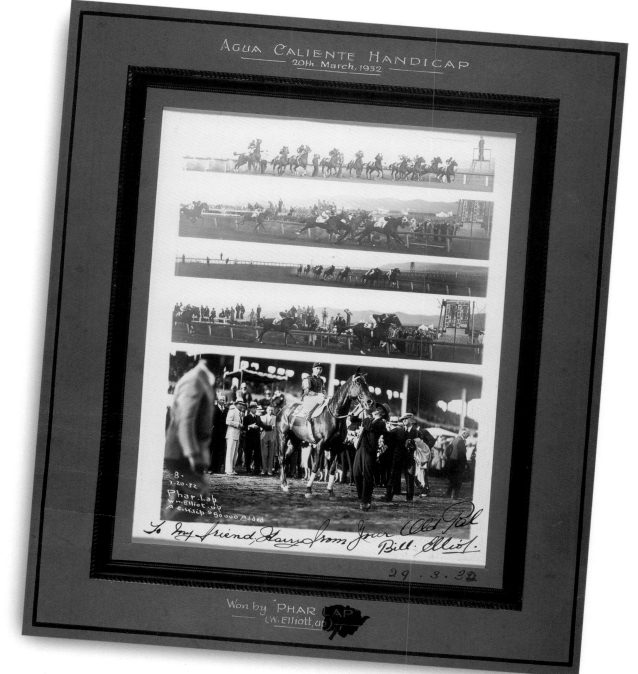

AGUA CALIENTE HANDICAP
20th. March, 1932

Won by "PHAR LAP"
(W. Elliott, up)

needed his attention. So it was decided that the 26-year-old Tommy Woodcock would be officially promoted to trainer for the trip.

Another important part of the success story who didn't venture overseas was Jim Pike. After a treacherously rough voyage to England as a teenager, where he left the ship at Colombo and returned home, Pike swore never to leave dry land again. Telford instead employed the services of Bill Elliot, who had won all six of his races on Phar Lap. Elliot took the distinctive saddle that Telford had made for him, specially weighted to compensate for his relatively light weight of 6 stone 4 pounds (40 kilograms).

On 17 November 1931, after a short rest at Bacchus Marsh, Phar Lap boarded a train for Sydney. The voyage to America was to be broken into two parts, with over a month's rest in New Zealand before continuing on to California. The Americans were not covering the costs for the first part of the journey, so his trip back home was a fairly substandard affair, travelling in the ship's hold with a motley collection of four-legged creatures, not at all worthy of the track idol he had become. Still, it was with great fanfare that Phar Lap was loaded onto an old steam-powered cargo ship, the *Ulimaroa*, on 20 November, in front of a large crowd of well-wishers.

Five days later, they arrived safely in New Zealand to a hero's welcome from a nation who had not forgotten, nor would let Australia forget, where the champion was born and bred. Phar Lap settled in well at his temporary home on the Trentham property of Telford's brother Hugh. During his time there, like any celebrity, he drew a constant stream of admirers who wanted to catch a glimpse of the local 'boy' made good. Woodcock was gracious enough to let his charge make regular appearances, and even allowed children to have their photographs taken sitting on Bobby's back.

With the transportation costs to California now covered, Telford was able to go to town on making sure that Phar Lap's journey was as comfortable and as stress-free as possible. The ship he was to travel on was the much newer *Monowai*, and Telford arranged for three enclosures to be built on deck, the largest six by eight metres, so that Phar Lap would have plenty of room to move and regularly exercise, ensuring his arrival in peak condition. Two of the enclosures were floored with coir matting, while the third had a layer of sand enabling him to roll around safely whenever he felt the desire. He had a 'state of the art' padded horse box to sleep in, which was also light and airy, a world away from the hold of the *Ulimaroa*.

In mid-December, veterinary surgeon Bill Nielsen and apprentice jockey Jack Martin sailed on the *Monowai* from Sydney to New Zealand. Just as they arrived, potentially disastrous news was received. Due to financial difficulties caused by falling attendances and betting revenue, the Agua Caliente Jockey Club announced that it was temporarily halting its racing calendar, which consisted of six days a week right through to the Agua Caliente Handicap in late March. Davis was on tenterhooks over Christmas until it was announced that racing would recommence on New Year's Day, and the Handicap would take place, but with a reduced purse of $50,000. Davis wired through to Woodcock that Phar Lap's journey to America was on again.

The troupe set sail for San Francisco on the *Monowai*, each provided with a comfortable and well-appointed cabin. However, it was soon apparent that Phar Lap became agitated when Woodcock was out of sight, so taken was he with his former strapper, and Tommy had to move his belongings and spend his nights sleeping in the horse box — not that he minded at all, as he loved the horse like he would have loved a friend.

The ship docked in San Francisco on 15 January 1932 to be greeted by Davis and the American media who had already labelled Phar Lap as the Red Terror and the Anzac Antelope. Although a little unsure on his feet after almost three weeks at sea, he seemed to have arrived in perfect shape, a testament to both Telford's preparations and Woodcock's care and attention from the time they had left Sydney. He then spent 10 days at a nearby ranch at Menlo Park to acclimatise before the road trip to Mexico. He was growing his winter coat, which Woodcock clipped (and which can still be seen on him today). Two days and 1000 kilometres later, Phar Lap arrived at the legendary Hipodromo del Agua Caliente resort.

The resort had been built to take advantage of Prohibition, the period from 1920 to 1933 when the sale of intoxicating liquor was banned in the United States. The rich and famous of California, including

Page Twelve *Agua Caliente Serenaders, of radio fame, in the Casino Patio*

Visitors enjoyed the lavish surroundings of the Agua Caliente complex, and were entertained by the best artists Mexico and the United States had to offer.
MUSEUM VICTORIA COLLECTION

the Hollywood elite, flocked across the border to drink and gamble at its casino or nearby racecourse. With the Depression reducing crowd numbers and biting into profits, the Agua Caliente Jockey Club saw the importance of attracting the best horses they could, so it is no wonder that the Australian wonder horse was high on their list.

Phar Lap was soon in his new quarters, specially chosen by Woodcock to be as far away as possible from the prying eyes of the press. As well as wanting to protect Bobby from too much commotion, he was under instructions from Davis to keep the horse's exceptional ability as big a secret as possible, in the hope of attracting the best odds when Davis made his typically large wagers. Phar Lap was exercised in the dark in the early hours of the morning and was only ever walking by the time the sun had risen. His first public appearance was to be at an exhibition race in early February, which was unexpectedly cancelled at the last minute by the Australians. It was only a week before the Handicap that the crowd got their first look at the champion when Davis and Telford relented and held an exhibition run around the Agua Caliente track.

Little was made public about Phar Lap's condition, until it was announced a few weeks before the race that his right front hoof had developed a crack after one of his early morning runs. Agua Caliente was his first experience of a dirt track, and it was during a run to accustom him to this surface that a pebble had lodged itself between the hoof and the shoe. The Americans were mistrustful of this statement, suspecting that the Australians were attempting to talk down his chances,

This horseshoe was reputed to have been made for Phar Lap to wear on the dirt track at Agua Caliente. After the horse cracked his hoof, Woodcock had to have another special shoe made to support the break.

MUSEUM VICTORIA COLLECTION
PHOTOGRAPHER: JOHN BROOMFIELD (MV)

resulting in favourable betting odds for them. Elliot, Martin and Nielsen — like Davis — all loved a flutter, and had been making the most of their time at a legal casino, 40 years before Australia's first one opened.

The hoof injury was real, though, and Woodcock and Nielsen worked frantically to have Phar Lap ready for the big race. After other attempts had failed, Nielsen took the drastic measure of cutting out the loose piece of hoof, while Woodcock had a respected Canadian farrier forge a special shoe which had a bar to help bridge the missing section. In the week preceding the race, the success of this, as well him being in peak condition, was made public knowledge, and Phar Lap's odds shortened to 6-5 to become the favourite. By then it no longer mattered to Davis, as he had already laid bets at the much better odds of 4-1.

Race day arrived on 20 March, with a full day planned as a finale to the Agua Caliente calendar. The Handicap was scheduled for late in the afternoon as race 13, making it a long day for the crowds of brightly dressed Mexicans and handsomely garbed American glitterati. Australians were able to listen to the day's events via a radio broadcast, sponsored by the Vacuum Oil Company, of variable quality due to the limits of technology at the time. The almost fanatical fixation by the Australian media with all things 'Phar Lap' in the lead-up to the race ensured a record listening audience around the country.

Eleven horses lined up for the Handicap, which was delayed due to Reveille Boy refusing to enter his starting box. Phar Lap was in box 9, an outside barrier, and was one of the last off. Elliot had planned it this way, so that the rest of the field were unable to box the horse in along the fence. Instead he sat comfortably at the rear of the field, Elliot purposely riding him out wide to avoid the dirt being thrown up by the front runners. It wasn't until the back stretch before the final turn that Elliot made his move, and Phar Lap hit top speed and flew past the rest of the field. It was their turn to eat his dirt!

Coming around the home turn, Elliot again restrained the equine powerhouse, enabling the other horses to momentarily catch up with him. Reveille Boy even managed to challenge him by getting a head in front. Elliot had the last laugh; with little more than a gentle nudge from him, the powerhouse was again unleashed

and they both took off and passed the winning post two lengths in front of Reveille Boy. The 50,000 crowd went wild — the Red Terror had come from across the globe and beaten the best the Americas had to offer, and in record time.

Phar Lap calmly walked to the winner's circle, though Elliot was less tranquil as he leapt off, grabbed the announcer's microphone and yelled, 'Hello, Australia! Hello, Mother! Your last letter spurred me on. This is a great victory!' A floral tribute was offered by two Hollywood actresses, which spooked the horse enough to cause him to strain a leg tendon trying to get away from the unwanted garland. Whilst the 1930 Melbourne Cup win had been Telford's to savour, this victory belonged to Davis who celebrated most of that night at the casino where the crowd was entertained by actor and singer Al Jolson.

Phar Lap was now the third greatest stakes winner ever, and Davis was adamant that his horse would give the first and second place holders a run for their money as invitations poured in from race clubs across the United States. There was even talk that Hollywood was interested in taking the Phar Lap story to the silver screen, so his entourage headed back north to San Francisco, resting again at Menlo Park, before deciding on their next move. For over an hour each day, visitors were permitted to see him, such was the interest generated by his extraordinary win at Agua Caliente. Although Woodcock was a little concerned by Bobby's slightly listless condition at times, nothing would prepare him, his colleagues or the American and Australian people for the tragic events of 5 April 1932. ❧

The Daily Telegraph

THURSDAY, APRIL 7, 1932

TRAGIC "LAST POST" FOR MIGHTY PHAR LAP SHOCKS

After news of Phar Lap's death reached Australia, local newspapers were filled with dramatic headlines such as this one.
Daily Telegraph, 7 April 1932

E THOUSANDS WHO LIVE FOR THE TURF, and the usands who can't tell a thoroughbred from a cab-hack— Australia has reason to mourn, the swift end that came to

could never be paid his owners than the comment heard on all sides: "Phar Lap was never 'dead' in a race!" and they spoke of his victories. Fifty-one starts meant 37 wins, three sec-

wins. Bought in New Zealand as a yearling, he held second place in the world list of stake-winners. He was Australia's ambassador in America, getting us what

money that Australia needs so iente win is estimated to have land, and the coming Americ

CHAPTER 5

Phar Lap's Last Post

The day dawned quietly at the Menlo Park ranch, Phar Lap's temporary home since his win in Mexico two weeks earlier. Phar Lap had seemingly been in perfect health the day before, 'performing' for an appreciative audience of over 1500 fans. However, he seemed far from perfect this morning, as Tommy Woodcock entered his stall around five o'clock to find Bobby in distress. Woodcock ran to get Nielsen, who diagnosed the symptoms as the early stages of colic. The pulse was a little fast, but the temperature was normal and stayed that way until around noon when it shot up to 102 degrees. By now, Phar Lap was showing signs of extreme distress and was obviously in a lot of pain. Nielsen no longer thought it was colic — now he was considering the possibility of acute poisoning.

He rushed off to the nearby Tanforan racecourse to find Caesar Masoero, the local equine vet, as Woodcock slowly walked the horse around the paddock. Phar Lap's condition was deteriorating rapidly, he began staggering, and was led back to his stable where he soon collapsed in an exhausted heap. Tommy cradled his head in his arms, stroking his mane, before Phar Lap began haemorrhaging fluid and then, around two o'clock in the afternoon, closed his eyes for the last time. Woodcock sat there in stunned silence, unable to believe that his Bobby was gone.

Nielsen and Masoero didn't arrive back at Menlo Park until after Phar Lap had succumbed. They received permission from Davis to perform an autopsy on the horse, finding his stomach and intestines severely inflamed, in a condition known as acute enteritis which was consistent with poisoning. Had this been caused by eating leaves from trees on the ranch which had been sprayed with a lead-arsenate insecticide the previous week, or by something administered by more sinister forces?

Another autopsy held four days later at the University of California came to a different conclusion. It ascertained that Phar Lap had been suffering from a colicky condition which also results in the acute inflammations found afterwards. Had this been caused by eating damp feed the day before?

The inconclusiveness of these reports only added to the heightened air of suspicion and intrigue. The nation was in disbelief as reports began filtering back that their hero was no more. Headlines declaring simply 'Phar Lap Dead' were soon followed by the uncertain 'Phar Lap's Mystery Death' or the blunt 'Phar Lap Was Wilfully Poisoned', as many Australians came to the conclusion that he had been murdered. The lack of any real motive or of any proof did not stop people saying in 1932, and still saying today, 'The Yanks couldn't beat Phar Lap, so they killed him instead'.

Over the years since then, a number of investigations have been held into a possible cause of death, as the evidence has been pored over and re-analysed repeatedly. It wasn't until 2000, when a group of equine specialists examined the autopsy reports in detail, that the most

probable cause was revealed. They concluded that Phar Lap had died from duodenitis-proximal jejunitis, an acute enteric disease of bacterial origin. This disease was unknown in 1932, and was not formally identified until the 1980s, but its symptoms closely align with those of Phar Lap's last day. Its mortality rate is still over 70 per cent so, even with the best of care, Phar Lap had little chance of survival. The stress involved with global travel and climatic change may also have increased his susceptibility to the condition.

As debate raged about the cause of Phar Lap's death, tributes and accolades were heard across the country, and across the world. Prime Minister Joseph Lyons declared that it was 'a great sporting tragedy'. Journalists, poets and other writers struggled to find the words to encapsulate their emotional response, and that of the nation, to this tragic event. Telford himself proclaimed the horse 'an angel. A human being couldn't have had more sense. He was almost human; could do anything but talk. I've never practised idolatry, but by … I loved that horse'.

RIGHT: After the initial period of mourning had subsided, questions were publicly raised regarding the mysterious circumstances of his death. Some were forthright, such as this one, suggesting it was no accident.

MUSEUM VICTORIA COLLECTION

OPPOSITE PAGE: Phar Lap's tragic demise shares the front page with news of the reopening of the Victorian state parliament.
Sun, 7 April 1932

He and his wife were inundated with dozens of condolence letters from grieving fans, as if they had lost a close family member. One wrote, 'I felt as if I lost my only child', and another, 'My sorrow today is as tho' I had lost my dearest friend', so great was the depth of their feelings for 'their' horse. Some requested photographs, shoes or even hairs from their beloved Phar Lap, as a cherished memento of his time on earth.

One writer from Tasmania suggested that the feelings of anguish were not just terrestrial: 'It rained here for a whole week, and I feel quite sure that the skies even wept for him'. The heavenly analogy was taken to the extreme by Joseph Fleury whose two by four metre painting *Phar Lap Before the Chariot of the Sun* depicted him leading the chariot of Roman sun god Apollo, surrounded by figures from classical mythology, including a cameo appearance by the recently deceased diva Dame Nellie Melba as one of the nine muses. It went on public display, with copies available for devotees to take home and hang on their walls as a personal shrine to their hero.

Meanwhile, Davis and Telford had to decide the question of Phar Lap's final resting place. As soon as word of his death spread, museums and other institutions contacted

"PHAR LAP BEFORE THE CHARIOT OF THE SUN"

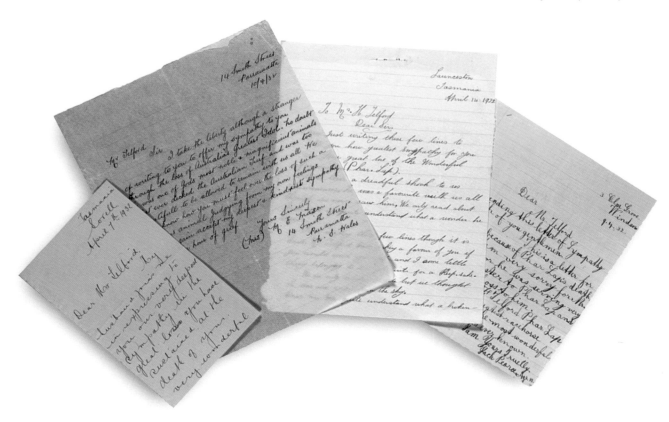

the owners in the hope of acquiring a relic from the remarkable creature. Only two days later, on 7 April, Daniel Mahony, Director of Melbourne's National Museum, wrote to Telford: 'In common with everyone in Australia I was shocked to hear of the sudden death of Phar Lap on the eve of what promised to be a triumphant racing career in America. If you have not already made other arrangements, may I suggest that his skeleton be presented to the National Museum for exhibition'. Although the skeleton proved to be unavailable, could Mahony have known that the result of his request would still be evident at the museum over 70 years later? ❧

ABOVE: The people of Australia responded to the news of Phar Lap's death with an unprecedented outpouring of grief, reflected in the many sympathy letters sent to those close to him, such as Harry Telford. A selection of these was donated to the museum in the 1990s by the Telford family.
MUSEUM VICTORIA COLLECTION

OPPOSITE PAGE: Tasmanian artist Joseph Luke Fleury employed a neo-classical style to immortalise Phar Lap in his painting, *Phar Lap Before the Chariot of the Sun*, 1932. The work was publicly exhibited and devotees could take home their own print of the painting. The original cannot be traced and these prints are now the only record of the work.
MUSEUM VICTORIA COLLECTION

A number of professional and amateur artists used their skills to capture the spirit of Phar Lap. *Riding Phar Lap*, an oil painting by noted artist Stuart Reid, was owned by the Telford family, and remained in their possession for almost 70 years.

CHAPTER 6

The Legend Lives On

Phar Lap accomplished much in his short but extraordinary life, and a nation grew to love him both for what he did and who he was. His owners knew that they were unlikely to ever see another horse quite like him and that his legend would live on in the years to come. With the horse assured of such a place in history, they decided to celebrate him by having him preserved by one of the top taxidermy firms in the world, Jonas Brothers of New York. Renowned for the realism of the lions, tigers and other wild creatures they had created for such distinguished institutions as the American Museum of Natural History, they were the ideal artisans to preserve the wonder that was Phar Lap.

Jonas Brothers spent over four and a half months working on the assignment, including two months studying the movement of horses at a nearby racetrack. Using the latest techniques to achieve as realistic a likeness as possible, they sculptured a paper and burlap shell supported by a wood and steel framework, over which rope veins were pasted, followed by Phar Lap's trademark chestnut hide, and finished off with the insertion of his ears, tail and mane. From the moment people first saw the finished creation, it was acclaimed as one of the most exceptional examples of the art of taxidermy, with one journalist noting that it 'truly reflects the commanding presence of Phar Lap in life'.

Although the National Museum in Melbourne had originally requested his skeleton to be displayed alongside those of other prominent racehorses, including the legendary Carbine, this had already been promised to Wellington's Dominion Museum (now the Museum of New Zealand Te Papa Tongarewa). His abnormally large heart, weighing six kilograms, was also unavailable, having been dispatched for examination at the University of Sydney and then deposited with the National Institute of Anatomy in Canberra. The institute's specimens later became part of the collection of the National Museum of Australia, where the heart is still exhibited.

Victoria was instead offered the recently mounted hide, which had been transported back to Australia and overwhelmed a crowd of onlookers, including a visibly moved Tommy Woodcock, when it was unloaded at the docks in Sydney. The offer was made in a letter from Davis's representative in Australia in early December

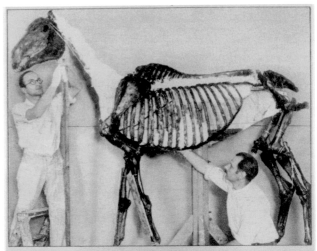

1 **Actual Bones of Phar Lap** are assembled as the first step in rebuilding his big body. The skeleton is put together with wire and steel rods. Thin plaster is then applied to both inside and outside of the skeleton . . . Phar Lap was believed poisoned, but an autopsy revealed stomach ulcers.

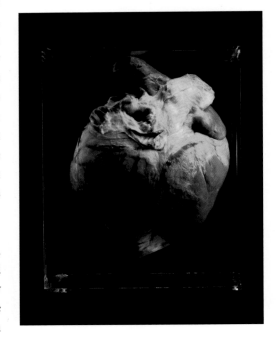

OPPOSITE TOP: Such was the significance of the project, Jonas Brothers of New York documented the preparation of the Phar Lap mount in a series of detailed photographs such as this one showing the first stage of the complex process.

MUSEUM VICTORIA COLLECTION

OPPOSITE BOTTOM: Phar Lap's heart.

NATIONAL HISTORICAL COLLECTION, NATIONAL MUSEUM OF AUSTRALIA PHOTO: GEORGE SERRAS

BELOW: Phar Lap's skeleton on display at the Museum of New Zealand Te Papa Tongarewa.

MUSEUM OF NEW ZEALAND TE PAPA TONGAREWA (CT.00997/02)

PHAR LAP at *Paramount's* **Capitol** *Theatre Magnificent*

Startlingly life-like —see the mounted hide of Phar Lap —just as he appeared on the track —a triumph of the taxidermist's art.

The Management of Paramount's Capitol Theatre have made arrangements that patrons of the MORNING—AFTERNOON and EVENING performances will have the privilege of viewing PHAR LAP in the foyer of the theatre, at the first exhibition in Melbourne.

By special request from many horse enthusiasts—the film of Phar Lap winning the Agua Caliente Handicap will be shown. Shows commence at 11 a.m., 2.15 and 8 p.m. For reserves phone Cent. 11085.

CLIVE BROOK and all star cast in "THE NIGHT OF JUNE 13"

ABOVE: Newspaper advertisement promoting Phar Lap on display in the foyer of the Capitol Theatre.
MUSEUM VICTORIA COLLECTION

OPPOSITE PAGE: As soon as he was installed at the museum in Swanston Street, Phar Lap attracted crowds of admirers who were keen to pay homage to their hero.
MUSEUM VICTORIA COLLECTION

1932, stating that 'the Taxidermists has made an excellent job in mounting him, and has also advised us that with proper care it will last a hundred years'. Although the museum was keen to accept the donation, an anxious letter followed a few weeks later requesting an urgent reply to the previous one, on the chance that the museum wasn't interested and another home had to be found. Fortunately for the people of Victoria, an affirmative response to this letter was promptly dispatched.

Phar Lap arrived at the museum in early 1933, after a three week showing at the Capitol Theatre in Swanston Street where thousands paraded past him. The imposing sandstone building which the museum shared with the State Library and National Gallery was his home for the next 67 years, as he became part of the fabric of Melbourne life and a treasured icon for the museum and the whole of Victoria. He was originally acquired by the museum as the pinnacle of accomplishment of the breeding process for thoroughbred horses, but it was soon apparent to all that the hordes of people coming to see him were doing so, not to examine a specimen, but to pay homage to an idol. The inclusion of such a 'popular' and seemingly non-educational exhibit caused concern among those who saw this as totally inappropriate for a cultural institution. One wrote: 'I contend that this museum is not the proper place to exhibit a racehorse, more especially when it is known of the direct harm that it is doing in a cultural sense to the people of this state'.

However, his popularity did not overly concern many at the museum, including Daniel Mahony who believed that many of those who were enticed through the doors to see Phar Lap would stay awhile and explore the many other treasures on offer. Over the years it became a tradition for parents and grandparents to bring children to the museum to see the horse that had been their hero during darker times. Author and entertainer Barry Humphries vividly recalls an experience common to many Melburnians:

> When my father took me into town and he was not on business, we would often visit two places: the Museum and the Aquarium. At the Museum he would hurry past the paintings and the stuffed bandicoots and the mineral samples, and stop only before one exhibit — Phar Lap, the famous racehorse, who stood, impeccably stuffed, in a large glass case. There was always a small group of awe-struck spectators around this mysterious effigy.

Gallery Director or
'*This way to Phar Lap*', 1954
Melbourne artist Eric Thake
humorously captured
the exasperation felt by
National Gallery director
Daryl Lindsay at the hordes
of people who came to the
Swanston Street building
looking not for art, but for
a horse.

The way Phar Lap was displayed conveyed little of the place that he had occupied in the hearts of Australians and his importance to a people wearied by the hardships of the Great Depression. The public provided their own interpretation — crowds of visitors could often be found standing near him, reminiscing or recounting Phar Lap's achievements to anyone who would listen. The public became the story tellers and keepers of the Phar Lap legend, and it was not until the 1980s, and the establishment of its social history department, that the museum followed suit and resolved to present a more comprehensive 'Phar Lap Story'.

To put on such an exhibition, it began building up a collection of objects which could be used to convey this important story to visitors. Since then, over 300 Phar Lap related objects have entered the collections of Museum Victoria, many generously donated by long-time admirers or by those directly associated with him in life. His strapper Tommy Woodcock and the family of trainer Harry Telford handed over treasured objects carefully preserved for more than half a century. Tommy presented his collection in person in 1979, lovingly unpacking a large suitcase as he gazed up at his beloved Bobby for the first time since 1932. As he unwrapped each cherished memento, including the brown checked blanket that Phar Lap had been wearing when he died, his devotion to the horse was still evident after almost 50 years.

These thoughtful donations have been supplemented by purchases of important items directly associated with him, and with the accompanying publicity and marketing campaigns that swept Australia. The most significant

Although he received minimal formal education, Tommy Woodcock's letter to a Canadian fan, written just before the Agua Caliente Handicap, is surprisingly eloquent.

MUSEUM VICTORIA COLLECTION

was the saddle specifically built for jockey Bill Elliot and used by him in Phar Lap's last race at Agua Caliente. The value of sporting memorabilia has sky-rocketed in recent years, and it was only with the assistance of the Commonwealth government's National Cultural Heritage Account and Racing Victoria that the museum was able to keep this important artefact in Australia.

All these items now form the museum's Phar Lap collection, and are in constant use in the Phar Lap exhibition at Melbourne Museum, the Phar Lap website and other public programs which examine the important role he played in Australian society during his lifetime and

ABOVE: Suitcase containing Phar Lap's brush, crop, kneepad, bridle, reins and girth. Donated to the museum by Tommy Woodcock in 1979.

MUSEUM VICTORIA COLLECTION
PHOTOGRAPHER: JON AUGIER (MV)

LEFT: Lifelong Phar Lap devotee Marie Davie bequeathed her prized collection of treasures, including this scrapbook, to the museum in 2000.

MUSEUM VICTORIA COLLECTION

the position he has occupied since then. However, the star of the show will always be the horse himself. His importance to the museum is demonstrated by the fact that, even with the many requests to borrow him from institutions and events around the country, he has left its walls only twice in over 70 years.

The first time was in 1980 when he was paraded through the city to celebrate the 50th anniversary of his Melbourne Cup win, and then displayed in a temporary structure at Flemington for the duration of the Cup carnival. It was the kind of event that the museum is unlikely to ever repeat, as there is always the risk of damage whenever he is shifted. When the museum relocated from Swanston Street to the new Melbourne Museum campus at Carlton Gardens, the move was unavoidable. One cold August day in 2000, in the dead of night, Phar Lap was transported in a specially built crate, on the back of a flatbed truck, the one kilometre to his new home. Unlike during his successful career, no records were broken by this run as the trip took over five hours of careful manoeuvring.

Before this move, Phar Lap was thoroughly examined and x-rayed to ensure that he was in a proper state to be shifted across town. His internal structure was found to be in almost perfect condition. Jonas Brothers' prediction that the mount would last a hundred years fortunately appears to be a conservative assessment of the quality and durability of their work. Phar Lap, and his enduring legend, will be around to captivate and inspire visitors to Museum Victoria for many more years to come. 🌱

Phar Lap's move to the new Melbourne Museum complex in 2000 was a carefully planned operation, befitting the treasured museum icon that he had become.
PHOTOGRAPHER: ANDREW HOBBS

Racing Record

TWO-YEAR-OLD

DATE	PLACE	TRACK	RACE	DISTANCE	MARGIN	ODDS	JOCKEY	WINNINGS
23.2.1929	Last	Rosehill	Nursery Handicap	5½ fur.			H. C. Martin	
2.3.1929	Unpl.	Hawkesbury	Two-Year-Old Handicap	5 fur.			F. Douglas	
16.3.1929	Unpl.	Rosehill	Nursery Handicap	6 fur.			H. C. Martin	
1.4.1929	Unpl.	Randwick	Easter Stakes	7 fur.			J. Baker	
27.4.1929	1st	Rosehill	Maiden Juvenile Handicap	6 fur.	½ len.	7/1	J. Baker	£182

Unpl.	Unplaced
fur.	furlong
len.	length
1 mile	1609 metres
1 furlong	201 metres

THREE-YEAR-OLD

DATE	PLACE	TRACK	RACE	DISTANCE	MARGIN	ODDS	JOCKEY	WINNINGS
3.8.1929	Unpl.	Warwick Farm	Denham Court Handicap	6 fur.			J. Simpson	
17.8.1929	Unpl.	Rosehill	Three-Year-Old Handicap	7 fur.		8/1	J. Simpson	
24.8.1929	Unpl.	Rosehill	Three and Four-Year-Old Handicap	7 fur.			J. Brown	
31.8.1929	Unpl.	Warwick Farm	Warwick Stakes	1 mile			J. Brown	
14.9.1929	2nd	Randwick	Chelmsford Stakes	9 fur.		10/1	J. Brown	£200
21.9.1929	1st	Rosehill	Rosehill Guineas	9 fur.	3 len.	2/1	J. Munro	£913
5.10.1929	1st	Randwick	AJC Derby	1½ miles	3½ len.	5/4	J. Pike	£7135
9.10.1929	1st	Randwick	Craven Plate	10 fur.	4 len	5/4	W. Duncan	£2205
2.11.1929	1st	Flemington	Victoria Derby	1½ miles	2 len.	2/9	J. Pike	£4456
5.11.1929	3rd	Flemington	Melbourne Cup	2 miles		Evens	R. Lewis	£1000
15.2.1930	3rd	Caulfield	St George Stakes	9 fur.		7/4	R. Lewis	£75
1.3.1930	1st	Flemington	VRC St Leger Stakes	14 fur.	5 len.	1/2	J. Pike	£1691
6.3.1930	1st	Flemington	Governor's Plate	1½ miles	4 len.	4/9	W. Elliot	£749
8.3.1930	1st	Flemington	King's Plate	2 miles	20 len.	1/10	W. Elliot	£1112
12.4.1930	1st	Warwick Farm	Chipping Norton Stakes	10 fur.	2 len.	5/4	J. Pike	£747
19.4.1930	1st	Randwick	AJC St Leger	14 fur.	3½ len.	1/20	J. Pike	£2478
23.4.1930	1st	Randwick	Cumberland Stakes	14 fur.	2 len.	No betting	W. Elliot	£1457
26.4.1930	1st	Randwick	AJC Plate	2¼ miles	10 len.	2/5	W. Elliot	£1451
10.5.1930	1st	Morphettville	Elder Stakes	9 fur.	5 len.	No betting	W. Elliot	£325
17.5.1930	1st	Morphettville	King's Cup	1½ miles	3½ len.	No betting	J. Pike	£800

FOUR-YEAR-OLD

DATE	PLACE	TRACK	RACE	DISTANCE	MARGIN	ODDS	JOCKEY	WINNINGS
30.8.1930	2nd	Warwick Farm	Warwick Stakes	1 mile		10/9	J. Pike	£200
13.9.1930	1st	Randwick	Chelmsford Stakes	9 fur.	2½ len.	1/5	J. Pike	£1033
20.9.1930	1st	Rosehill	Hill Stakes	1 mile	1 len.	2/7	J. Pike	£597
4.10.1930	1st	Randwick	Spring Stakes	1½ miles	½ len.	1/10	J. Pike	£1467
8.10.1930	1st	Randwick	Craven Plate	10 fur.	6 len.	1/6	J. Pike	£1830
11.10.1930	1st	Randwick	Randwick Plate	2 miles	2 len.	No betting	J. Pike	£1465
25.10.1930	1st	Moonee Valley	W. S. Cox Plate	9½ fur.	4 len.	1/7	J. Pike	£850
1.11.1930	1st	Flemington	Melbourne Stakes	10 fur.	3 len.	1/5	J. Pike	£1000
4.11.1930	1st	Flemington	Melbourne Cup	2 miles	3 len.	8/11	J. Pike	£9429
6.11.1930	1st	Flemington	Linlithgow Stakes	1 mile	4 len.	1/7	J. Pike	£1000
8.11.1930	1st	Flemington	C. B. Fisher Plate	1½ miles	3½ len.	No betting	J. Pike	£1000
14.2.1931	1st	Caulfield	St George Stakes	9 fur.	2½ len.	1/14	J. Pike	£600
21.2.1931	1st	Caulfield	Futurity Stakes	7 fur.	neck	1/2	J. Pike	£2600
28.2.1931	1st	Flemington	Essendon Stakes	10 fur.	3 len.	No betting	J. Pike	£700
4.3.1931	1st	Flemington	King's Plate	1½ miles	1¼ len.	No betting	J. Pike	£700
7.3.1931	2nd	Flemington	C. M. Lloyd Stakes	1 mile		1/3	J. Pike	£200

FIVE-YEAR-OLD

DATE	PLACE	TRACK	RACE	DISTANCE	MARGIN	ODDS	JOCKEY	WINNINGS
25.8.1931	1st	Williamstown	Underwood Stakes	1 mile	1¾ len	2/1	W. Elliot	£350
5.9.1931	1st	Caulfield	Memsie Stakes	9 fur.	3½ len.	1/6	J. Pike	£500
19.9.1931	1st	Rosehill	Hill Stakes	1 mile	1½ len.	No betting	J. Pike	£444
3.10.1931	1st	Randwick	Spring Stakes	1½ miles	1¼ len.	No betting	J. Pike	£779
7.10.1931	1st	Randwick	Craven Plate	10 fur.	4 len.	No betting	J. Pike	£940
10.10.1931	1st	Randwick	Randwick Plate	2 miles	4 len.	No betting	J. Pike	£740
24.10.1931	1st	Moonee Valley	W. S. Cox Plate	9½ fur.	2½ len.	1/14	J. Pike	£500
31.10.1931	1st	Flemington	Melbourne Stakes	10 fur.	½ len.	No betting	J. Pike	£525
3.11.1931	8th	Flemington	Melbourne Cup	2 miles		3/1	J. Pike	
20.3.1932	1st	Agua Caliente	Agua Caliente Handicap	10 fur.	2 len.	6/4	W. Elliot	US$50,000

Pedigree Chart

Sired by Night Raid and foaled out of Entreaty, Phar Lap's five
generation pedigree indicated that the horse had some promise.

			Bend Or 1877	Doncaster 1870
		Radium 1903		Rouge Rose 1865
			Taia 1892	Donovan 1886
	Night Raid 1918			Eira
			Spearmint 1903	Carbine 1885
		Sentiment 1912		Maid of the Mint 1897
			Flair 1903	St Frusquin 1893
Phar Lap 1926				Glare 1891
			William the Third 1898	St Simon 1881
		Winkie 1912		Gravity 1884
			Conjure 1895	Juggler 1885
	Entreaty 1920			Connie 1884
			Pilgrim's Progress 1889	Isonomy 1875
		Prayer Wheel 1905		Pilgrimage 1875
			Catherine Wheel 1891	Maxim 1884
				Miss Kate 1873

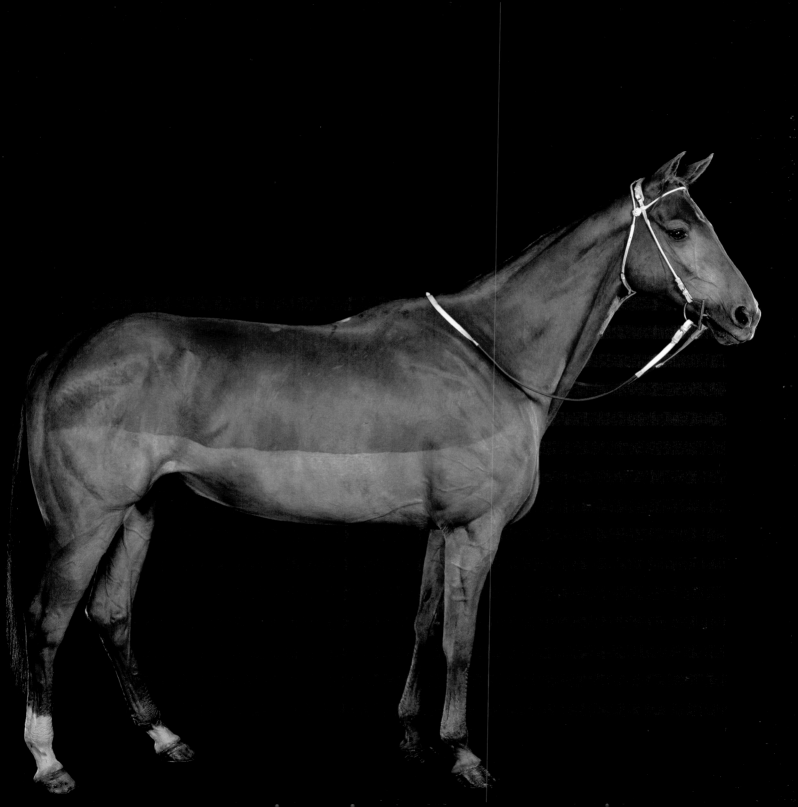